SURVIVOR'S GUILT

ANTHONY RODRIGUEZ

Survivor's Guilt ©2022 by **Anthony Rodriguez**. Published in the United States by Vegetarian Alcoholic Press. Not one part of this work may be reproduced without expressed written consent from the author. For more information, please write V.A. Poetry, 643 South 2nd Street, Milwaukee, WI 53204

Cover art by Jessi Carrubba

for you

YOU TAKE A SUMMER

digital cake, thunder, and you are missed. Letters without meaning. You were told that saying fosters. You feel this assumes you've said before. You don't know.

You see yourself in the middle. All those colors you chose and allowed to stay. The rooms in your ears haven't agreed in months. You find that your days little loudly,

YOU HASTILY CUT OTHERS FROM YOUR LIFE
22

YOU FUMBLE AN OMELETTE OVER AND END UP MAKING SCRAMBLED EGGS AND IT STILL TASTES FINE BUT IT JUST TASTES FINE
73

YOU GO WHERE YOU CAN BUT DON'T AND DO MORE OFTEN BECAUSE THIS IS TRUE NOW AND WON'T BE

piss. Mustard, bagel, you pull out a confusing map. You turn this sideways. *Nothing*. You take this map to you. You read this map and ignore you watching you read.

You hate going to you.

You ask for today's summers.

You went through most of your summers earlier.

Bodyguards throw you out across the pavement.

And the map is gone!

Double fuck! A drum circle out of bad habits. You invite longer conversations this way. You stare yourself up and down. Tie die, carpet, rats. You're covered in scratches. You're missing an arm. You find and wear it across you. You just want to get by. You consider.

Xanax, fluoxetine, seroquol,

YOU WATCH WORKOUT VIDEOS AND PAUSE THEM WHEN YOU HEAR NEIGHBORS
34

YOU PLANT A MAGNOLIA IN THE MIDDLE OF THE BACKYARD AND IT FEELS LIKE SOMETHING BIGGER HAPPENS
7

YOU PLANT A MAGNOLIA IN THE BACKYARD AND IT FEELS LIKE SOMETHING BIGGER HAPPENS

middle of the day

YOU MOVE FUNITURE BECAUSE THESE ARE THE CHANGES YOU FEEL YOU NEED TO FEEL NEW
12

YOU PREPARE FOR WEEKS
60

YOU SLEEP FOR TEN HOURS AND USE THE BATHROOM AND DRINK A GLASS OF WATER AND SLEEP FOR ANOTHER TWELVE

as you lay for twenty minutes. Plywood. Mist.

This song smothers you with last summer. This makes you tired. You find an outlet and just start pulling plugs in hopes to get you to stop. You yank at piles and piles of plugs.

You find your plug buried under these. You spend summers watching yourself. You complain and find it holy.

You survive you around you to practice this watching.

You trip over you, stiff, march, middled. You shatter

YOU CANCEL YOUR ATTENTION TO RECHARGE
40

YOU ORDER YOUR DREAMS ONLINE
29

YOU WEAR MISTAKES

cords that launch you into the sky, holes in the ceiling, tabloids. Gambling circles. Tofu. Pallets, taste buds, coats, yesterday laid eggs and left them for the house. A love note attached. You throw these at you. Summers stream from shells.

Cucumber leftovers.

Hummingbirds. Gruel. You pass you in cells. You were told to avoid eye contact with you. *You'll find a way if you let you,* you say. Your face riddles with light. You start with one outlet and follow the current. You ask you to move as needed. You mess with this and blacken the house. *Whoops.* Jars and bottles jot from the ground. This treasure rumors to other houses. You invade you in pursuit.

You find an oasis and stay here. You fight on. Jellybean. Bank.

Noon gives you head. Tomorrow and yesterday come home together. You run on wheels. Each step dreams.

You wake up after you already left. You announce this with compassion. You forget with zest.

You tell you that one day is each day.

Then you let you out the back door.

You flirt with freedom. You find another house and foresee a connection between the two. A network, ska, helixes. A republic, jeans, washes over. You find you find you in others. Galleries of porches. Foundations curl and squish over summers. You adjust. You find a house in the yard and yank at it. The tree tears up wiring where roots would run.

This rips the house inside. The house is just happy to be included.

You're electric. You burn through yourself. You radiate who you look for. You take pride in powering the house. You feel you work well together to mean stability and security. You know you try. You now need to try differently. Moth, daisy, anthill, magnets, you do. The house weathers the excitement. You train to prepare. A cigarette rolled with a petal.

You're over it. Because fuck you.

You shop for you in baskets. You tell you what kind of you you are. You're sold. You buy one one day and two another. You decide to share you with you. You feel special. Then ten houses collapse onto this one. Thousands grow like weeds. You spend summers controlling spread. These are one of many. You think little at this rate.

You think about leaving. You let routines take you around the house. You feel you've thought enough.

Summers spill from bottles. Light stirs like frost. You bet all your hope on a giant sling shot. Red. You play the wrong game. You'll be back tomorrow.

You work any work you can. You share stories with those around you. These float and fly

YOU UNMATCH WHAT'S MISMATCHED AND REUNITE PROPER PAIRS **45**	**YOU MUNCH TELEVISION SHOWS** **79**

YOU WASTE AN OPPORTUNITY

arms onto your bed. Industry. Your libido on the fridge with magnets. Tomorrow is overdone, and you'd rather have something else anyway. Cold. Together for warmth.

Barely.

You boil houses for meals for summers. You feel you've grown tired of houses and summers. You feel you're all you have. Wanting stops with you.

Your hair against candlelight, melting, spilling into honey at your ankles. You serve dinner through its rising. You tell you about your day.

Conversations up to your chin stretched high.

Your tongue flirts.

Sky eats glass

YOU FEEL THE SUN IN BED AND FIND A GENTLE GRIP
49

YOU STRETCH YOURSELF WITH THE WEEK AS THE WEEK ASKS FROM YOU
42

YOU WASTE AN OPPORTUNITY
11

YOU DELETE ALL THE ALARMS MEANT TO WAKE YOU UP
48

YOU MOVE FURNITURE BECAUSE THESE ARE THE CHANGES YOU FEEL YOU NEED TO FEEL NEW

tie a rope. You tie this summer tightly and cut it with today's light. You make cassettes and cd's out of your routines - things that can do things, things that can be things, and things that can do/be things with things. You build radios out of summers. This radio tunes into last summer and next summer. You find you most of all. You get lost trying to get you to be until you forget why you do this. You mostly just do to do and forget.

You mostly feel you mostly just watch.

Villain.

You spearhead a plan for you. You only care about you.

Houses howl.

You learn sign language to get by. You misunderstand you. You fight. *Oh jeez*. The house loses houses. The neighborhood ripples with wind. You feel pretty. Stop betting it all

YOU HAVE A NIGHTMARE AND RUN OUTSIDE UNTIL YOU CAN'T RUN ANYMORE AND YOU WATCH THE CITY FROM A BENCH
41

YOU SIGN UP FOR CLASSES AND CANCEL THE DAY OF
13

YOU SIGN UP FOR CLASSES AND CANCEL THE DAY OF

it. The sink fills with sky. You feel focus. Conditions stain and wash off in the wash.

You flood into the room just to see. You pluck houses from corners and wisp parts into the wind.

You spit seeds. You press the first few into the floor. You let the rest just fall where they lay. Screws blossom. You accidentally cause mass destructions. *Shit.*

New clothes.

You see you in the mirror and tomorrow when you close your eyes. Parry.

You remove a wall to see the houses running the house with wire and wheels and labor. You join. You train. You love you by the time you're ready.

Everything is so different than when you first started.

Fish swim.

Wonder.

Light.

Houses panic. You left. How.

Shit's stupid.

You're stupid.

Because fuck you.

Rupture. Melon taffy.

Red velvet

YOU HASTILY CUT OTHERS FROM YOUR LIFE
22

YOU GIVE YOURSELF A DUE DATE FOR YOUR LONELINESS
43

YOU DRINK TOO MUCH

over your shoulder, and, soon, you rip you out of the water. You fling. You take your time preparing you, cooking, asking how you can make you better. You come in and tell you to do something about the smell. You open the window next to you, and summer haunts you. Gardens are poems. One hundred million you climb through. You overstuff the house until you explode with you.

Heartbreaks, handfuls of blueberries

YOU LEARN TO UNWANT THE THINGS YOU FEEL YOU WANT
51

YOU GO WHERE YOU CAN BUT DON'T AND DO MORE OFTEN BECAUSE THIS IS TRUE NOW AND WON'T BE
6

YOU PRACTICE DRAWING SHAPES WITH YOUR EYES CLOSED FOR WEEKS AND LEAVE THEM OUT FOR YOURSELF

if you were too cowboy. This summer stirs the house, spinning since morning. You swim across rooms and pretend what's happening isn't really happening.

You leave. This summer snows.

The house dials, and you count how many times you see the front door. You only see lights on in the windows, and you can imagine what's inside. You see you smoking a cigarette and feel inclined to tell you about it. You ask if you can just smoke a cigarette, please. You take a sip from summer and spend summers

YOU ALMOST TELL SOMEONE YOU'VE LOVED THEM FOR A LONG TIME
57

YOU NOTHING AND NOTHING ELSE
82

YOU SLEEP OUTSIDE TO CHIRPS AND WAKE WITH BUG BITES

chalk, you hear there's a monster in the house. You're on edge. Just be better.

Streetlights as blankets. Nothing. Nothing. *Twenty million, please.*

Bells who swing with life. Age as texture. You slip on something in the hallway and below the floor. You gaze the house through glass. Routine aquariums. You poke and try to evoke change. You get hungry. You eat yourself.

The house catches wind and puts a ping pong table down there. Seeds when you talk. Mood rings. Duct tape. You see flowers bloom from the wall. You learn to try to keep them around. Giving gives you energy. You ate all the fucking tomorrow again and left you with an empty box. You slap you silly. You mistake you for you. You slap you for revenge, and it quickly becomes a slap fest. You trust you'll tire out and get there eventually. You make breakfast for when you wake up.

Yesterday makes this drudge.

Summers of quitting because fuck this and fuck you.

Basil butterfly wings.

Trash bags, fun. Automatic payments. You make lists for summers. You feel you find you when you cross things off. You hunt for these feelings across the house. You find similarities between you and you. You feel somewhere in the middle. You find a house on the floor, shake you into your hand, and lob you as wishes. Trauma engine

YOU SPEND HOURS ON THE PHONE WITH SOMEONE YOU MISS
46

YOU SLEEP FOR TEN HOURS AND USE THE BATHROOM AND DRINK A GLASS OF WATER AND SLEEP FOR ANOTHER TWELVE
8

YOU BUDGET ENERGY FOR DIFFERENCES YOU WANT TO SEE

that you tell the sun moon things. Most probably things you guess, and guesses grow into beliefs. Belief is a ladder made of flowers. And there's a run that's just beyond the memory of growing and grown guesses.

You know you'd just get through it if you left it to you.

And you're elsewhere. *Of course.*

Just gone.

You throw a fiesta. You have a mix cd playing music. You point a lot. You lead a dance line through a crowd. Froth and study. The house is brighter than bright.

Patience for a kind of forever. Double hell. You nosedive into yourself. You live as if the things that might happen will never happen. Fog collapses around a building.

You peek at you and see you being you for the moment, and, in that moment, you tasted how bad it was to be with you to drag you down. You remember the magic in every slice of ignorance.

There's a very hard reality that you're made aware of, and it's important to remember that you're working within the context of that world.

You collect houses from the garden. The house asks for so many, more than you can make. You just love your houses, in your hand, admiring how much you've grown in such a short amount of time.

Summers of summers of permission.

Leaks, rubber paste, sun light curls into hearts over

YOU TAKE IBUPROFEN FOR THE HEADACHE THAT FINDS YOU
64

YOU LEAVE CHANCES TO DRY
78

YOU TRY TO CLEAN THE PROMISES YOU BROKE

even though you've given yourself days to stop being you. You feel a part of you will always you. You feel you'll you less. You feel this less you will lead to not you. You read this from science from the house. Rooms read other sciences in other houses. You see little success.

Summers filled with your favorite summer. You feel a small energy between your teeth. Garbage cans, flexing. You pick these. Your mouth is struck, damaged – energy, tossed and broken about.

You try to unplug you standing over this mess. Summers of oceans of wires plague the house. You guess at each mess by looking for paths.

You bless the house with babble. You run to each room. You swear you say each word the same each time in each room.

Conditioning, twine, barking dogs. You find that most words change as you say them.

So you quit, because you're done.

Your game is broken.

Because fuck you.

You go back to your day. It grabs you, and you forget the whole thing. You're back where you were. *Fuck.* Then you get better more and more until you now live in a stable part of the house and try a moderate enough amount to survive and to have a life you can enjoy. You look back and feel you never would have imagined. You love now always. Rabbit, ribbit. Hundreds of houses knock on the door and you try to provide. Everything collapses immediately.

Oops.

Summers of fall. You mostly get by. You made a good support system over the years. You feel lucky in such a way that this system is built in such a way where seeing them feel natural. You look forward to your time with you.

Creek, dull apple slices. Afternoons for summers.

You love how the hours look in jars. You admire. Light cross-stitches. You're drunk off some summers. You help you to you who know you. You leave you. You tell you a week later. *Fuck,* is all you offer. You take it as one of those things.

You look forward.

You remember how easy things are again and you often remind yourself to hold onto it this time a little bit longer, you idiot.

You shout over at you trying. You fight. No one tries

YOU FORGE A NEW PERSONALITY
83

YOU FUMBLE AN OMELETTE OVER AND END UP MAKING SCRAMBLED EGGS AND IT STILL TASTES FINE BUT IT JUST TASTES FINE
73

YOU HASTILY CUT OTHERS FROM YOUR LIFE

tarantula. You find you ruined this night months ago. This hits you weeks later, cold, already two weekends deep.

You speak into unspoken space
.
You swat at hours around you.

You follow a map to your bed.

You swamp the space in bed in piles.

You know there's no room for you.

You were once told that your bed deserves you.

This idea creeps onto dinner in front of you.

Avoiding this idea avoids this bed avoiding you.

Because you're not hungry anymore.

Because fuck you.

Tunnels and ring tones. You bend yourself into sounds. You fill your hands with these and carry them to outlets. You plant these ideas into each socket and pray for

YOU COUNT ALL THE RATS THAT RUN ACROSS THE STREET
69

YOU PRACTICE DRAWING SHAPES WITH YOUR EYES CLOSED FOR WEEKS AND LEAVE THEM OUT FOR YOURSELF
16

YOU SPILL SECRETS INTO A FAN IN A ROBOT VOICE

your questions about your survey. You had to make a few more efforts, then you would just be on probation. You need at least today's payout. You take this as reason to get to tomorrow. You take that as an invitation to do small things you enjoy that you never quite have time to do.

You gain enough energy to get through it, and that's all you can ask. Turkey bacon, refusing what's around you holds you back. Because fuck you. Grape smiley faces. Summers of smiley faces.

You question things. You approach you and introduce yourself as a doctor and ask if you can study for science. You promise money. You mention it's forever.

You're put through the works. You're told you could help you by becoming medicine to treat you. You're asked to think about it. You help those around you, and, alive, you're choose to live. The house inflates. The house has fun keeping this in the air for summers.

You see out the window. You see and know you're a place you can get to. The light is energy, and, with running water, feeds everything. You feel it's fun to feel like you're going somewhere. You get distracted by the day. The house hums.

Sometimes you sing along.

Gravy, you hear you can summon you by magic. You try an

**YOU THINK ABOUT
KILLING YOURSELF
37**

**YOU GO TO A BAR WITH
A FRIEND AND TALK
ABOUT HOW YOU BOTH
USED TO BE DIFFERENT
39**

YOU WAKE UP TOMORROW

the time to get to you. You feel only a part of you holds your breath. You get into what you've built to be a car made of cardboard.

You watch the cardboard city squeak with pulley. This space allows you to imagine a life with you. You tip you. The city outside this city runs through you.

You come back more frequently and for longer than you care to admit. You move on because you have to. Because fuck you. You still feel everything feels backwards.

You're everything you say you are. Then not at all. You try to get back there.

You feel the need to try differently. You try to feel the need to try differently.

You feel you need to try differently to try to feel the need to try differently. You try to feel the need to try differently to try to feel the need to try differently.

You feel you need to try differently to feel the need to try differently to feel the need to try differently. You try to feel the need to try differently to feel the need to try differently to feel the need to try differently.

You feel you need to try differently to feel the need to try differently to feel the need to try differently to feel the need to try differently. You try to feel the need to try differently to feel the need to try differently to feel the need to try differently to feel the need to try differently.

You feel you need to try differently to feel the need to try differently to feel the need to try differently to feel the need to try differently to feel the need to try differently.

You walk through a scene and feel great your life isn't your life.

You mistake you for the kitchen curtain, blowing from the window. You just want to be close to you. Because, for a half of a second, you are, you feel you must be. Light trucks through the house. You're enraged.

Blind, you fight.

You crumble in a short period of time.

A pinch of today on today already made. Summers of fucking whatever this is. You share this with you. You pass plates all across the house. You're taken aback when you get yours. Tomorrow gets rowdy. Yesterday calls. *Jeez*. You try to find today. You take today's attention. You

YOU FUMBLE AN OMELETTE OVER AND END UP MAKING SCRAMBLED EGGS AND IT STILL TASTES FINE BUT IT JUST TASTES FINE
73

YOU HELP A NEIGHBOR MOVE A LARGE DRESSER AND YOU NOD A LOT BECAUSE A LANGUAGE BARRIER
74

YOU REDECORATE AND REORGANIZE

laugh tracks. You fold into cracks in the walls. Each a boardinghouse filled with desperate slivers.

You try to visit this place less. You take up dance lessons. This room is overrun by you. You lose yourself somewhere in the house for summers.

Loop, volcano, acceptance.

Finally.

Except you can't choose. You stick with thinking about choice. The day begs for you. You have accidents while your attention is away. Summers of debt. Vivid, baseball, pudding, your days spin on your finger. You try and lose interest quickly. Time, alligators.

You figure that a coat of paint covers mistakes. You do this until you physically can't move.

You find you also in the day. You're surprised how much you miss you. You feel this tells you something. All the stairs to get home feel fewer.

You feel you should do something today.

You pull one over on you. You have folders, cities of hope, keeping plans. You ask you for help in your materials. Everyone together to pull one over on you. Because fuck you. Tonight is a curse word. You find energy in bedtime stories. You like to fade while holding onto something. Work changes. Life changes. The house folds.

Orange

YOU BUDGET ENERGY FOR DIFFERENCES YOU WANT TO SEE	**YOU SEE MOVING TRUCKS STUFFED WITH HOPE**
18	**44**

YOU TAP INTO MEMORIES AND BREAK A VALVE

the church bells. Grain. Fresh colors. You find yourself in pets. You take you for walks around the house. You come across fountains every few feet. You take these moments for yourself, sitting, imagining the wishes you threw before, stretching. These parts of the house make you forget the house. You come up to you and ask you if you've seen you.

Today, it's easy to say no and move on. You visit these places for weeks. You study what gets fixed, how often, and when. You see you make repairs with parts of yourself. You're struck to see you this way. Your moments are eaten when you look away.

You offer to help you if you help you. You don't feel that's fair. You glare at loss. The day swarms.

Houses for dinner. Summers to swallow what little you can.

You sweat forever in seconds. You jump to keep these in bottles. Conveyor belts drag these to other houses. Bottles keep energy alive. Tarot, cantaloupe. Ant, fever. Sparklers.

You find conversation in stacking houses together in your head. When it's too full, you drag them into shapes. They form what you aim for. You trickle in gather to notice. You offer interpretation. You give guidance. Grace. To apply these together, you find you have to remove sound structure. You offer corrections. To apply these, you find you have to remove yourself from

YOU HASTILY CUT OTHERS FROM YOUR LIFE
22

YOU SPILL SECRETS INTO A FAN IN A ROBOT VOICE
23

YOU SPEND A NIGHT THINKING ABOUT THE DAY AFTER WITHOUT PANIC AND WITHOUT FEAR AND WITHOUT CONCERN AND WITHOUT JUDGMENT AND WITHOUT DOUBT

into your life to bring out the best in you. Whatever it is, you see to it how you know how. Gravity sycamores. Forever seeds. You lie down in a double yummy sandwich. You feel you've made it wrong. You feel it's a little off.

You're allergic to you. You're doomed.

Summers sneezing. You're sick of you. *Ew*. Blue awe. *Gosh*.

Two hundred houses sneak under the house. They adapt. You infest the house. You have to call you to exterminate. You believe this is a task you accept as a part of life. You proceed coldly. You have one less problem. Today slept in, yesterday calling. You feel confined in this space. You sing your woes to the afternoon. You feel they're better off on their own.

Light paints ponds that stretch across the house. You graffiti over this. Because fuck you. Mute music.

Doves, iron. Bad touch. Garnish. The house detoxes. Breaded greeting cards. Acting class.

You fire you. It's one of those days. You throw you out. You'd rather be somewhere else anyways. There, you wonder what else. You help you hang laundry on electrical cords. These

YOU PICK FLOWERS AND HOLD THEM TIGHTLY
67

YOU COUNT HOW MANY WEEKS IT'LL BE BEFORE YOU HAVE TO HAVE CHANGED COMPLETELY
55

YOU WATCH THE PHONE RING
65

YOU ORDER YOUR DREAMS ONLINE

too late again. Tomorrow hogties the next day. You kindle a fire that roars with houses. Each house whines as it chars.

You feel you just need a break. You hear you in your head. How just a couple of houses becomes just a couple hundreds of houses quickly.

You remember when you used to you.

Flowers coast.

Mornings under you.

Who you used to be gives you energy for the day in ways you wish summers would. You try to you from memory. You feel that if you could replace every you with you, you'd be alright.

Light needles records. The day sounds like days. You plug chords back into their sockets. You feel you have to believe in you. Hiccups. Granola.

You weave wires into blankets. Tread

YOU GIVE YOURSELF A DUE DATE FOR YOUR LONELINESS
43

YOU STUDY WHATEVER FEELS LIKE CAN BE YOU
56

YOU THANK THE DAY

over. Around, even throughout. Under the roof, foundation begins to shed. Summers of cleaning.

You grow anxious as it's near done. You wonder what else when this is over. It's minute season. You flick them from your arms and legs. You find they're worse in some parts of the house.

You take turns with medicine. This makes them friends. You and everyone and the house cheer beautifully.

These songs keep you awake at night. The roof disappears. The world goes downstairs through your bedroom.

You talk yourself out of bed. You charge a fee. You ask the sun to leave.

When you get home, you sleep for moments, which, soon, you're told were months. You're surprised how easy it is to return. The house folds into an airplane. It loses a race with other houses. You like how the day plays this way. For summers, your bones become lights. You unplug you. You feel lost. You search for a spot to sleep again. Because fuck you. You feel it makes sense to start again.

You make everything new.

Casserole. Barbed wire. Geese, musk. Tan. Spice. Tomorrow glows. Harmonica. Cliff. Paths. Stale afternoon.

You pass waters out to you. You drink these faster than summers, under your breath. You use light as encouragement. You teach you how to farm.

Sideways.

You save your life. You become best friends. You move away.

You change because you changed.

You've missed calls from today.

You take surveys. You find it impossible that you hate everything. You feel you're sure. Fried anguish for

YOU PICK FLOWERS AND HOLD THEM TIGHTLY
67

YOU TRY TO FEEL LIKE YOURSELF
38

YOU COME BACK EVERY DAY

beehives and wheat toast, trombone shine. You reach for yourself around the bend. You catch some part, and you fumble out just as quickly.

You miss these games.

You haven't found yourself in months.

You can't help but be so close to finding you soon.

Because fuck you. Because you've been training.

You're sure you have your number.

You're not sure you won't because you're not even aware.

You're too busy tossing a house into the microwave. You slip a dash of houses before you notice. Today asks you what happened yesterday. You fumble. You tell today that you and yesterday always kept to yourselves. Your house is done.

You deep sea dive through the grass yard.

Thick energy.

You forgot how boring everything is.

You find brief excitement in having found this. A deep sadness around your neck. Paint and baseball bats.

You wait in line to watch you watching. You're behind twenty you. You feel as though this line moves every summer. You forget why you wait, but you sure know you have to keep going. You feel sudden determination means something.

The line pretzels across the house.

You doubt this line leads to you. The house is full of hopeful hermits. You rant about last summer freely.

You wonder how you can make you notice.

But you're too busy, wild with mercy, stuffed with summers.

You consider that you only notice you when you notice you.

You feel no notice when you wait to notice you.

You find the map in your arm. You guess at the country inside. Tacos,

YOU REDECORATE AND REORGANIZE
26

YOU ASK FOR HELP
80

YOU WATCH WORKOUT VIDEOS AND PAUSE THEM WHEN YOU HEAR NEIGHBORS

spinach, you scowl at the lines already. Within minutes, lines behind you. You're in the middle quickly. Even yesterday is smashed. Chicken sandwich. Salad, gunpoint. You become business. You melt in splashes for summers to fuel a machine. Then magic - bellies full of you.

Summers of leftovers. You feel you're too much sometimes. You forget when you settle.

You throw away what can't be stored. You fill garbage cans. You cause a smell. You complain. You desperately switch gears to a joke.

Summers of set up,

YOU DRINK TOO MUCH
15

YOU HELP A NEIGHBOR MOVE A LARGE DRESSER AND YOU NOD A LOT BECAUSE A LANGUAGE BARRIER
74

YOU SPEND AN EVENING WITH PEOPLE YOU LOVE

is fortune is an aggregate. You earnestly propose a pragmatic condition about yesterday. Understanding as the fourth dimension. Professional wrestling, the fifth. You float away from the house, excited, lifted in front of your face. You see you dangle, and blow at you out of sight. Because fuck you. You invent the solution to everything that you left to ruin in the wash. None of you know you or what the fuck you're talking about. This day slobbers. The whole house runs slower than usual. You can see this on a monitor. You pluck a tin can from the wall and report this.

Fuck

The other houses are kicked into fractioned extra work.

You were tossed outside. A three-month fall. You hitchhike as far away from home. You think you see you come back one afternoon. And you weren't sure.

You eat your thoughts from a bowl. You drop by with candlelight and a blanket for your shoulder. You wear this for summers. You never remembered a candle. You live out long enough for you to grow from you. Farms of fields filled with you. You whistle on windy days. You spend nights dreaming. *Wow*, you mouth.

Practical jokes for a living. Lots of plastic, lots of rubber. You kick your head off! You bring a community together through sport. You honor you with a wreath, a firm handshake, under your breath - *Thank you. Thank you for kicking your head off.* You cheer and feel alive again. Handprint gravy. Tootsie, stove. Summer sandwiches for summers. You lick these days, trusting it won't melt on your hand. This invites years.

Years and years of this shit. You finally get a turn at the end of your line. You step forward and forget what the reason for waiting your whole life was. You laugh. You all laugh together. This house buzzes in the house. You find it - *Finally* - and smash it. Breadcrumbs

**YOU TAP INTO MEMORIES
AND BREAK A VALVE
27**

**YOU SPILL SECRETS INTO A
FAN IN A ROBOT VOICE
23**

YOU THINK ABOUT KILLING YOURSELF

even if all tomorrows are gone, you wonder if you hear the heat in your words. Light sucks. You close the curtains. You study you for summers. You write a manual about how you behave and why. You're tried for treason. You integrate this into law. You act differently, and you feel like you're back where you started.

Because fuck you.

Hundreds of holes through you. Houses chew. They spill out, trailing in pathways. They spring and bloom bright with houses hanging with droop. Your holes stay the same, and you feel it's beyond you anyhow.

Blame is loudest.

Holy shit. You just leave all this. It's that easy. You exit the house. You walk away.

You remember you have to let you out. You go back. You know, tomorrow really would be a better day anyways. You come back. You're so glad to see you because you missed you.

Frogs. Muscle memory.

Number, banana, rifle, you spin houses on your finger. The universe bounces under a table. You'll get you later. Houses grow.

You block the sun. You

YOU THROW OUT TRASH AND CLIMB THE FENCE TO HAVE A DRINK WITH YOUR NEIGHBOR WHILE PETTING THEIR DOG
62

YOU PREPARE TO BE CRUSHED BY FAILURE
58

YOU TRY TO FEEL LIKE YOURSELF

You unplug you and climb into the socket. What you fill the day with aims. Weather is a dull blade.

You sweat ghosts.

These ghosts kiss your cheeks. You're ready. You see all your hard work going at it without light. Summers of work. You cave at an accident. Summers of acceptance. You make a house that burns when you plug in the toaster. Teacup overalls. Bend wagon. Tornados, internships, you find energy in studying you while studying you. You find tomorrow in being on your toes. This game for summers.

The house happens around you.

You take photographs of you in the house. You find things that are funny. You sweep with all your heart. Thumbtacks, you keep moments as bookmarks. Dill pillows. Garden hose. These color pages. You pick at them while in line to make a cheeseburger. A fight breaks out. You take part until you're a pile of body parts. You're taped together. You all find peace in light in the afternoon.

Trees grow into rooms of the house, and you know enough to make rooms in these trees in rooms of the house. When you're finished, you ask you what took you so long.

Bath water. You move on with the day. It laces between your fingers, and you nestle together. You forgot all about you.

Red suns scour across the sky

YOU SLEEP OUTSIDE TO CHIRPS AND WAKE UP WITH BUG BITES
17

YOU WEAR MISTAKES
9

YOU GO TO A BAR WITH A FRIEND AND TALK ABOUT HOW YOU BOTH USED TO BE DIFFERENT

squashed yellow jacket pale to blue.

Cartoons. The one you're thinking of.

You chuckle a few times tomorrow for having held this. You take your energy and feel it doesn't work for you. You throw it away. You feel lucky you hold so many wonderful things in front of you: today, right now.

You're alright. Helium.

While you taunt you while you struggle to get over

YOU TRY WHAT OTHERS HAVE SAID
61

YOU DON'T FEEL LIKE YOU AND YOU CAN'T MAKE YOU HAPPEN
53

YOU CANCEL YOUR ATTENTION TO RECHARGE

apologize to apologize for apologizing. You catch up on intuition. The conveyor belt in the living room keeps you awake. You rotate from one end to another.

You take beyond you, past recommended, just to fall asleep. You don't care how much you it takes. You swallow you either way - summers full of you full, hoping

YOU COUNT HOW MANY WEEKS IT'LL BE BEFORE YOU HAVE TO HAVE CHANGED COMPLETELY
55

YOU FUMBLE AN OMELETTE OVER AND END UP MAKING SCAMLED EGGS AND IT STILL TASTES FINE BUT IT JUST TASTES FINE
73

YOU HAVE A NIGHTMARE AND RUN OUTSIDE UNTIL YOU CAN'T RUN ANYMORE AND YOU WATCH A BUSY STREET FROM A BENCH

light barrows quickly, tucked in a room with you there, shocked. It murmurs a mild mango. You carry this with you.

A syringe sucks the house and all of you into tubing. You inject you with some you. A line of you leads you to you. You say this is a vaccination, for protection. You don't know from what. You just follow these instructions.

You walk from this line to another line. Then that line over to that there line. Then there, if yes, and that way if no. If at any point you are unable to comply with security restrictions in a timely manner, then you go back. And you don't want to go to that line.

Gosh. You just go and try your best. Eh. The house is onto other things more worthy than your attention. Ouch.

Summers in motionless stir.

Age covers you. First as dust. Then as dirt. Then life. Then a small tree. You wake up and pick up what's left with growth on your side. You feel it's what you do - just heavier.

You wait to be you in another line of you. God, speed, stutter, clouds

YOU COME BACK EVERY DAY
32

YOU ORDER YOUR DREAMS ONLINE
29

YOU STRETCH YOURSELF WITH THE WEEK AS THE WEEK ASKS FROM YOU

make sure there's a little summer in you every evening. You swing for summers that stay longer and longer.

A magnifying glass to this summer and light and you. You freeze this in the freezer. You wait for the right moment. Polaroids of change you were too distracted to see. *You have to pay money for this shit?* You feel it's hard not to hate you when you do stuff like this.

You run simulations for what went wrong. They find light and fight you because it feels right. You have mixed feelings. You debate. You build a republic. You just drink.

Stall.

Nightstand.

You grate compliments into shreds. These shreds trickle. Summers shape. You surround your self in arms. You close your eyes. The day takes you. You cup your hand under faucets. You whisper to water. Time drowns

YOU GIVE YOURSELF A DUE DATE FOR YOUR LONELINESS
43

YOU SPILL SECRETS INTO A FAN IN A ROBOT VOICE
23

YOU GIVE YOURSELF A DUE DATE FOR YOUR LONELINESS

into different days. Feeling stupid, you shut down the fight you build in your head. Each day is cancelled. Each day with glue. Summers molt while you pluck flowers from your foot. Sometimes you take out a lighter and watch the day melt over your hand. Sometimes you mosh your fucking brains out.

This abuses meaning, and trust is the train you take. Houses hail. You sneak away from you and all this shit and the house and you go eat some pizzas downstairs, sunk into basements, holding oceans. *Great*.

The house grows hair. Trees peel.

You try to forget your head. You feel stuck. You dig yourself from the middle of you and break out of your head. You find you waiting for you, and, in this

YOU DRINK TOO MUCH
15

YOU DON'T FEEL LIKE YOU AND YOU CAN'T MAKE YOU HAPPEN
53

YOU SEE MOVING TRUCKS STUFFED WITH HOPE

you never are. You smell campfire, picking minutes from the carpet. And in this fun you feel loss. You trace today over today. You keep these in empty summers.

Last summer lasted these summers to bruise the rest of today. You grab you while you run. You go with, you feel this means you've been waiting for this.

You rip you out of your mouth. *Get out*. It's about leaving yourself. You believe you're you. Waves and waves of belief.

Belief as an accessory. You're out of season this summer. You have a hard time working together.

You've made a hobby out of putting you in bottles. You keep you in a drawer in the fridge. The collection stares at each other, mostly taunting. A fair enough resistance to address: you

YOU TRY TO CLEAN THE PROMISES YOU BROKE
20

YOU THROW OUT TRASH AND CLIMB THE FENCE TO HAVE A DRINK WITH YOUR NEIGHBOR WHILE PETTING THEIR DOG
62

YOU UNMATCH WHAT'S MISMATCHED AND REUNITE PROPER PAIRS

the end of you. You slip tirelessly your mouth.

You sigh one big sigh. Pigeons.

You watch you through this window. This means you have a vantage you're unsure what to do with. Ghosts, toasts, and roasts. You tell you in passing. You hear you sell this information and disappear. More and more of you disappear always. You feel you can only believe things as they are. You never know. Leaflets. Batter.

Houses line up in the house.

You're taken away by you. You knew you would know where you came from. You drink gallons of houses to investigate.

You say you won't get away with this.

You might as well help. You hate you too. Because fuck you.

Cigar smoke. In each house, every summer, you you. You look for you in crowds. You ask look for you inside you, and you're pulled over to the windows in your gut. Theatre chairs. Safety

YOU MUNCH TELEVISION SHOWS
79

YOU STRETCH YOURSELF WITH THE WEEK AS THE WEEKS ASKS FROM YOU
42

YOU SPEND HOURS ON THE PHONE WITH SOMEONE YOU MISS

sleepless, opinion, cookies, gut. Rosemary, time, carpet designs. Mythical creatures, autobiography, pasta, shorts, drain cleaner, laundry detergent, picture frame.

Summer sweeps.

Popcorn, dice, cinnamon rolls, receipts, change, exposure.

Hamper, fitted sheets, the cities that ask for you, puff, mushrooms, umbrella, copper.

Dandruff. Pizza boxes.

Stuffed animal, book ends, utensil, lemons, toothbrush, cereal, dandelions, chickweeds, dog shit, moth, popsicle, vinyl, anal, cell phones, instruction manual, you treat you with you.

You exit the control console as you shut down; a small crew exit your pods. You check in enough for summers after. You feel like duty. Rim shot, you mostly just want to forget.

Cities cry out.

Dynamite, performance, relic, tantrum, you feel you're always in the middle of your own shit, custom, treadmill, finches, emergency, fun.

You sculp an army out of clay. Summers give you control. You resist. You spend summers trying to understand yourself because you also would want you to try to understand you. Moons gossip over you.

You feel hopeful for the future.

But you betray you! *Drat!*

You agreed only to be able to trap you. Your strength surprises you. You leave because you feel no reason why you should stay. Raspberry tart. Tea.

The day grinds. The house using another kind of communication. If you visit, you feel you have no reason to adapt. Breakfast sampler. Coffee and whisky.

Houses coordinate a dinner party. It's pretty cute.

:)

You gather at windows, struggling to see what happens next. Maybe

YOU LEARN TO UNWANT THE THINGS YOU FEEL YOU WANT
51

YOU SPILL SECRETS INTO A FAN IN A ROBOT VOICE
23

YOU DELETE ALL THE ALARMS MEANT TO WAKE YOU UP

scissors. You feel you know you enough to know what happens next. You pinch houses over the afternoon. You cut your finger. You call your replacement. You became a crisis worker because you love jumping into action. Grand slam, milk. Hundreds.

You can imagine. You on film.

Old everything. New nothing.

You spend yesterday in last year.

You short circuit. You call you to fix you to replace you. You say this happens more than you think. You ask how come. You shrug. You unscrew screws. You tug at fistfuls of wires in your belly. You charge more money than you have. You break you and offer to come back once you do.

You relieve you. Your problems are your problems now. Because fuck you.

The house on speed dial. Voicemails. Order numbers. Today blushes. You massage answers out of walls. You write these as history. You learn. You contest. Waiting.

Your head, spaghetti, hangs with weight.

You fall asleep when you fall asleep. Tomorrow with cream. The year, black. Oceans brim

YOU THANK THE DAY
30

YOU FEEL ALONE
50

YOU FEEL THE SUN IN BED AND FIND A GENTLE GRIP

tomorrow tastes funny. You check the date and smell spoil. Even after you throw this out, it lingers. You know it'll be there. You're told that some things in the house are meant to be thrown away.

Exhausted consent.

These summers spoil anyhow. You put these in the backyard. You wander off on your way. You come across a place before openness. You sit here. Today is whatever the fuck this is. You watch you become part of everything outside. A bee buzzes. The house behind you catches fire. You're in it. You're the fire

YOU MUNCH TELEVISION SHOWS
79

YOU GO WHERE YOU CAN BUT DON'T AND DO MORE OFTEN BECAUSE THIS IS TRUE NOW AND WON'T BE
6

YOU FEEL ALONE

about falling houses, happy accidents, tragedies. These kindle across rooms. You get together and make a plan to protect the house. This involves trust.

You're too diplomatic. Something happens at the same time you take you on a date. You forgot you could be like this. Something happens at the same time tonight whisks.

You make scrambled eggs out everything. You feel it tastes alright. *Whatever*.

You expect little. Moon erasers.

You swat minutes for summers. You overhear with scrutiny. You feel compelled to remind you who you are. You already have little energy to fix what you already need to make up from yesterday for. You digress. You trust you and keep doing your part.

Minutes go by, harmless. You continue on about the day after. Light conducts the hours. Sometimes you listen.

You swim through worry. You ask you to tell you something. You pass this along and see how this nothing to you means something to you.

You invite you for dinner as thanks. You learn how you live differently. "This is my life," you remember you saying, gesturing towards you. You paint this moment from memory. A series more detached. A lifetime of reaching. Sugar squares.

Summers are low this summer.

You tie bows around you as a hobby. You feel honored when you ask you

YOU TRY WHAT OTHERS HAVE SAID
61

YOU DON'T FEEL LIKE YOU AND YOU CAN'T MAKE YOU HAPPEN
53

YOU LEARN HOW TO UNWANT THE THINGS YOU FEEL YOU WANT

makes you jump.

Shouts explode

across the house,

an ocean of disapproval.

The daylight shutters

from the window and sprawls.

You instead split yourself into

groups: those in light, those in

between. You always find

yourself in the middle.

You have work to do

to get back to you –

work that's more than

just you. You in light

and between light clap

in unison. You shower

in sound. The floor burns.

You fall out

**YOU STUDY WHATEVER
FEELS CAN LIKE CAN BE
YOU
56**

**YOU HELP A NEIGHBOR
MOVE A LARGE DRESSER
AND YOU NOD A LOT
BECAUSE A LANGUAGE
BARRIER
74**

YOU DON'T FEEL MUCH LIKE YOU AND YOU CAN'T MAKE YOU HAPPEN

drilling into you. You glitter chasms. Light fills the house. Some remember. Some forget. You're reminded about choice. Tomorrow finds you and asks for help. You go with it. You meander for summers. You walk through bottle oceans - thick.

You build. You shake houses into a fishbowl. You swim and pick at flakes. You fight for it. Some get some. Some get none. Patterns. You collect debt. You drag through the evening. You resist. You expected differently. Lounge.

Ginger. You notice your body in an open bottle.

You trade numbers to hold onto an idea. Last summer sighs. This blows over the neighborhood. White starks. You feel you chew nothing because you always had. You slip.

Summers strike you.

Harm pastes.

You push the house blocks over. Tides as high as the sun.

Light pours itself into the glasses you place.

You study this and plot how to intervene. You know, on some level, you feel you expect you. This means you prepare for you. This means extra. You turn summers with coffee each morning.

You find your plans have overgrown.

You use these as snacks, mindless, flavor, mixed with yesterday. You miss you. You find yourself in pulling outlines. You dribble into puddles. Rooms simmer, slush sticks to you. This summer caves in.

Catalogue.

Naps that curdle. You call your attention.

You have a hard time noticing when the house sheds.

You make plans. You change them.

Tornadoes whisk desserts from your mood. These harden over afternoons. You pick at one with each moment you don't notice. You hunt for these windows. They stalk.

They tape you, back against the door. You reach forward, never looking back. The night only lives

YOU COUNT HOW MANY WEEKS IT'LL BE BEFORE YOU HAVE TO HAVE CHANGED COMPLETELY

your dreams about kissing, and you kiss a summer from the fridge. You feel like you've lived long enough to know enough to die now. You poke at the world with bubbled riots. Rustic tension. You carry a private truth in your lower back, then a pushed tickle injected into your knees.

Tomorrow explodes. Sometimes you try, and you feel lucky if that means anything. A month of medication spills onto the floor. You sweep weeks into the dustpan. You find that not even your reward is rewarding.

The wind whips.

Pigeons dive one after the other. Most probably. You burn your fingertips in the toaster. You find a surge in questions you knew were there. You stick yourself in the fridge. Soon tomorrow will make shadows shake. You use you to the fullest, wide without breaking. Your loudest sound is an exhale. Then white, then you again. Fuck. You whistle and headbutt walls inward. Maybe you're still asleep this week. Jars suck sound

YOU WATCH WORKOUT VIDEOS AND PAUSE THEM WHEN YOU HEAR NEIGHBORS
34

YOU MOVE FURNITURE BECAUSE THESE ARE THE CHANGES YOU FEEL YOU NEED TO FEEL NEW
12

YOU STUDY WHATEVER FEELS CAN LIKE CAN BE YOU

feed onto the floor. You fumble the hallway with tongues and slop spoonfuls into the walls. You wipe your forehead, inhale this hour, think of summers to come. You've counted your days recently and made meaning from these numbers. Then meanings from meanings. You send smoke signals to the next shift with notes about the day. You feel most days are just the same day forever. You play cards with you until the next feeding. You come in with filled buckets. It always smells.

You work closely together. This pushes you into mouths. *Whoops*. The wall figures you out. You keep down the hall. You pet the mouth over your face: *good boy*. You receive a complaint about blocking you with you. *Extra in the way* was triple underlined in the report. You wander back into the living room to see where you last left your place in line for tomorrow. You wave frantically at yourself, stepping out of line to grab your attention. You scold you until you're bored caring. Then you both eat ice cream. You drop your spoon onto into foot traffic. You reach, and the current pulls you. You grasp for anything, and what you pull is a plug of plugs.

The house shuts down

YOU HASTILY CUT OTHERS FROM YOUR LIFE
22

YOU FUMBLE AN OMELETTE OVER AND END UP MAKING SCRAMBLED EGGS AND IT STILL TASTES FINE BUT IT JUST TASTES FINE
74

YOU ALMOST TELL SOMEONE YOU'VE LOVED THEM FOR A LONG TIME JUST BECAUSE

that again. This window passes quickly. You think of other windows before you. You wonder if the windows you climb into are worth climbing into in the first place. You feel swallowed by windows you overlook, and you're the window, and you're jumping out of it.

Fists. Houses sink into sinks.

Wow. Because you too.

Days take you for summers. Light clots between your eyelids. You try and quit again. You feel you don't have it in you to you again. You have to pawn what you want for what needs to happen. The house cooks lifestyles. You cut your hair differently. You find a whole house that accepts you. You nap in the windowsill.

Afternoons lull with fables.

You hear you left from you. You heard from you, and so on. Some houses move. Pancakes, hammocks bunk from the ceiling. Races

YOU NOTHING AND NOTHING ELSE
82

YOU SPEND HOURS ON THE PHONE WITH SOMEONE YOU MISS
46

YOU PREPARE TO BE CRUSHED BY FAILURE

knocking, of course, you enter your own head. It looks like you thought it would. You clearly see the problems. You explain the mechanics of this through that and you feel you're honest enough to quote an honest quote. You tell you. You feel it was a good deal. Crusty sun dials. Mint chocolate. French bread.

More sunsets. Summers of sunsets. Minutes on the floor again. Hours lost. You perform a concert. You turn the house down. You unplug it instead. You check the rest of the kitchen and mosey through the hallway.

Your alarm goes off. You work with how sensitive you are. Everyone's happy. This lasts the weekend. Tomorrow for dinner. Every. Night. You have leftovers in the freezer and discover you frozen.

You unfreeze you, and, with adjustment, you strive to re-freeze yourself because fuck this because fuck you. You feel determined to wait.

Pumpkins. Mulch. Kale.

Pale sugar. You feel people in line around you are just in the middle and with it with you. You stay in touch for years. Your house is crushed, and consecutively every house around. You use walkie talkies to investigate why.

It's you. You're shocked.

You say you were just mowing the lawn. One hundred billion you sue you. It doesn't look good. Ski trips on wishes. It's a place you visited, sits special, and carves a taste to share with you. Apple fritter. Sickness. Vans. Cacti.

Light teaches you classes. You take notes and talk about it with you. You argue. You push. You find resolve somewhere in the middle. When you ask light to lead you, you learn to work with you. You keep the fridge of bottles of light next to the fridge full of bottles of summers. You look for more energy under couch cushions. Street racing

YOU UNMATCH WHAT'S MISMATCHED AND REUNITE PROPER PAIRS
45

YOU FUMBLE AN OMELETTE OVER AND END UP MAKING SCRAMBLED EGGS AND IT STILL TASTES FINE BUT IT JUST TASTES FINE
73

YOU PREPARE FOR WEEKS

your favorite summer in a glass. You drink as though you're behind. You lose track of how many summers you swallow. You clog. You shuffle anxieties to pressure give.

You sweat from unplugging. Pushed. You find houses inside you. You reach deeper and find you. You keep this from you. The house would tear you to shreds. You deny summers. You watch change watch you closely. The house changes shifts. You sneak among lines. You hear stories that you found you. You rear years.

Suspicion is medicine.

Days charge.

You parent. You resist.

Because fuck you.

You never thought you would have to say these things to you. You never knew you had to not you to you.

The front window laps at horizons.

Rain shines drops that crawl.

An entire staircase up to your attitude.

You tuck your second guesses into the breast pockets of all the jackets you find. You grow outside of outside of

YOU SEE MOVING TRUCKS STUFFED WITH HOPE
44

YOU MUNCH TELEVISION SHOWS
79

YOU TRY WHAT OTHERS HAVE SAID

surrounded. Vibrations. You load for summers. You crush this whole waiting thing. You live proudly. That's it. That's all you do, and you get hired because you're the best. You go home and hope for tomorrow. This give you energy. The money is okay. You train a school. You lead you. The house drowns. You step on houses as large as crumbs. Because fuck you. Bean dip. You pour houses into plants each morning. You feel hope this time. Tomorrow takes yesterday home and asks you to look after today. *Fuck.*

Toothpicks, you love you too much. You ascend. You let go. The house is there when you get back. You live today like it always has been, knowing. An alarm goes off. Hot water boils the house whole. Canyons.

Family. You make mac and cheese for the whole house. Summers of mac and cheese.

Summers of wanting more eventually.

You run through neighborhoods through the house. You like to see you, who you are, who you aren't. You can stay away from home, and this keeps you. Home is mostly the scraps you have because it has to be. You grow and parent these into something stable. You're horses that run. You sprint forward. Purple puffs. You're always going

YOU STRETCH YOURSELF WITH THE WEEK AS THE WEEK ASKS FROM YOU
42

YOU WASTE AN OPPORTUNITY
11

YOU THROW OUT TRASH AND CLIMB THE FENCE TO HAVE A DRINK WITH YOUR NEIGHBOR WHILE PETTING THEIR DOG

screens with every house in view. Your best is shy. Coffee breath, bed frames, you're quickly replaced. You find out later you're always replaced. You think then for those stuck there now. You're unplugged for your salt lamp. You feel warm with companions. Terrorism. Crochet. Yesterday's late. You feel a little relieved.

Polaroids, roses, games that take you away. It takes you all day to get there and all night to get back. Summers to explain why it's worth it. Paddleball forevers. Everything and alone. Branches, river.

You drop you in a glass of water. You swelter with each second. You grow and keep growing. You grow into who you fell in love with all those summers ago. You saw you then. You break houses and houses. Houses conduct meetings about how to stop you. You can only get so much done with squeaky chairs and a stuffy room. You must delay, put in the order, appeal, and reschedule. Even summers are under construction. You feel you hardly get to the end of things.

Errand mountains. Hobby porn.

You put up posters on one side of the house while you pull them down on the other. The best part of your days are when you pass each other and can high five. You ask you what happened to you when you don't show up for work one day. You shrug and understand it as one of those things. You miss you.

Caricatures as public service announcements. Wooden water. Secrets are gravediggers asking for tips.

You formulated a system to have a line holder for every first person in line for each part of each day. You balance this, using as you need, trying to need less. This and everything you could ever want.

Because fuck you.

You taxi your summers around. You're sharp. You know stories. You'll take you here, there. You stammer in choice. You drop you off at a world when you're ready. Windows down. Syrup city.

Helmet. Back stroke, toast, misspelled diaries, apricot, cricket clock, mood, evergreen, juice. You lose your keys. *Darn!* You trace your steps from late day to mid-day and admire the number of things you did the second time around. Your keys are lost. Your car is stolen. You're lost in the crowd. You lose you.

You move on.

You find other places you're safe. Then these places are built over. You have to let go. You book a trip. You get there. You love it. The house is different when you get back and you don't give a shit. You have enough of yourself again to return. School plays. Mornings in deep stretch. You pick each other up, light cigarettes, and talk about how the moment passes. You've learned you never want to be the first one up. Then the day really begins.

You see a bird sputter from the window, into the room. It hops and chirps and jumps and searches about. It flutters there, there; there, noticing you, fumbles a way out. So quick for summers of guilt for being. These fill your pillows. They're all your furniture. They insulate the house. You inspect it one day, half-assed, pointing about. You try to check more what needs replacing more. You look forward to something other than summers to get through things. You feel this inherently means tomorrow. This diet

YOU ORDER YOUR **YOU PICK FLOWERS AND**
DREAMS ONLINE **HOLD THEM TIGHTLY**
29 67

YOU TAKE IBUPROFREN FOR THE HEADACHE THAT WILL FIND YOU

and you and light and not you and not light. You leave for a walk and find the house surrounded by teeth.

You say nothing about these days.
In your head, you scream for miles. These years tear

YOU FUMBLE AN OMELETTE OVER AND END UP MAKING SCRAMBLED EGGS AND IT STILL TASTES FINE BUT IT JUST TASTES FINE
73

YOU PREPARE FOR WEEKS
60

YOU WATCH THE PHONE RING

when you heard you, you thought of you. Summers drag you through each hour. Muscle honey, mildew. You bury your habits and find a hole in the ground. You peer into a house filled with you. You direct traffic.

You find faults in your fantasies for summers. You wonder if your faults have fantasies, and if they so far have been luckier than you in any way. This summer is turned on by consequence.

You echo across the neighborhood's lips. You dig a hole with your hands. You see you've managed to master a tunneling system, a meticulous harmony. You shout at all the bodies that scramble to get this done in that way and so forth. You pick you up. The sun cut shadows into your face. Because fuck your fucking face.

Your face for summers. No matter what.

You dangle you in sunlight, pinched by pant cuffs, reaching, grasping.

You hit your foot on something you know you planted there for you to find it. And you fell for it! *Darn!*

You hit you head and think hard. You fall into your own head for summers. Outside of you, you're snapping in your face. Shrugging, and waving with one hand while pointing down at you. Because you know you've done your job.

You know the look, and, with envy, you regain your own sense of purpose. You hold this close to you, tucked at your side, glowing. You can do whatever so long as this glow stays. You hum real close, a lullaby, pregnant notes. You unplug you, taking off your earmuffs cuffed with summers. You sigh because you know you've done your job.

You fly away forever. Gone. Great. Because

**YOU ALMOST TELL
SOMEONE YOU'VE LOVED
THEM FOR A LONG TIME
57**

**YOU NOTHING AND
NOTHING ELSE
82**

YOU PICK FLOWERS AROUND THE NEIGHBORHOOD AND HOLD THEM TIGHTLY

You tell yourself you'll only give up if you want to too. That way, it'll be your fault.

You don't have to be alone together.

You want a list of everything you do so you can memorize it. You draw your portrait, you're the prairie you're running through.

Some kind of apple that's part grass and part lemon.

A chase. Some reeling with whips, lashed. You almost fall asleep thinking about a life with you.

You find that if you just forget everything forever, then you're good.

You struggle deep in the arms of the afternoon.

Years and years of summers in these afternoons. You find a zipper in the window. You pinch this, pull, shatter shapes, and up to come together again.

You zip and unzip to see how even change has to change just as much as you do. You find where the zipper is only a splinter. You thank it endlessly. Because you don't know, and you can never know.

Fuck.

And then yesterday becomes today with today, and, together, forget about tomorrow for today. You remember that you were in the middle of something. Beyond yourself, you find freedom, wonders filling the room.

You knew everything would get better just by freshly painted room. You keep up this feeling by repainting. When you talk about life, you want to fuck you up. You leave you to boil for ten minutes. You mix in houses. The pot inflates with food, the hot rubber, your dumb leather.

Yeah, fillet. Fuck, salmon.

You cut up the evening into diced cubes, a little rectangular, and the sides some triangles. You set the moon to cool. You forget and find it too cold. You drink a coffee too late and another just for fun.

Where therapy is putting something in the microwave, the plate is too hot, the food is too cold. You stand up and tell that you're all wrong and that everything's great. Just seeing you requires permission. You remember how someone said being so happy could make you cry too.

Each summer each day crunches between the moon's bite. Time is only as exact as it's spotted; a pin in its name, all the names scattered. Cowpoke, reservoir, madness. You steer outwardly inwardly

YOU FUMBLE AND OMELETTE OVER AND END UP MAKING SCRAMBLED EGGS AND IT STILL TASTES FINE BUT IT JUST TASTES FINE
73

YOU MUNCH TELEVISION SHOWS
79

YOU COUNT ALL THE RATS THAT RUN ACROSS THE STREET

the last time you laughed so hard. You walk through a gallery of mistakes to get a phone charger. You return to the party. You had fun helping you. You took streamers and banners with instinct since you're excited about the glitter cannons and ice cream cake.

You see you hug you, high five, fist bump, kiss. You sing a song you know. Millions belt with might. The floor gets warm and starts to burn holes.

Walls crinkle.

You open gifts. You cut the cake. You think of a really great thing to wish for:

YOU COME BACK EVERY DAY
32

YOU SLEEP OUTSIDE TO CHIRPS AND WAKE UP WITH BUG BITES
17

YOU BUY BOOKS AND READ A FEW PAGES INTO THE TRANSLATOR'S NOTES

has lifted you and carried summers. You nail clothes to the wall. You fit yourself into these and pretend to pretend.

With you, you know you don't know. Ear drums, forgiveness, cock rings. The floor rises. You envy your heights, breaking you around you as you soar. You shatter. You gather.

You tell yourself that this is the third day. Always the middle of the week. You interrogate this truth until you forget you and the summer and the house and what truth you were looking for and sink into finding and wanting to find.

A spot in the house blocked by velvet rope. You bump into you, and you point to a sign – *only you*.

You tower through you and ropes.

You search the house for houses. You break the tiny doors and pour you into your palm. You approach you with your handful. You deny you, thumbs down.

Because fuck you.

You douse this night with days. You see you in the window.

You see blurry houses across from you.

You find that streetlights treat you better than sunlight.

You nestle under a table. You feel you've found a way to be happier with what you have. You wait summers to ask you how when you wake up.

You come back when you can. This grows to be hours every week, then days to months. You ask around after your efforts have no effect, and you tell you you've never noticed you. You hear you laugh in the other room.

You feel like you miss out on you, wrapped in your own shit. You help you out of the middle.

Rental spaces. Second interviews.

Lunch breaks. Smoke breaks.

You shake your hand. You take you with you. You can't afford you. Tensions rise. Things change. Things

YOU SPEND AN EVENING WITH PEOPLE YOU LOVE
35

YOU TRY TO CLEAN THE PROMISES YOU BROKE
20

YOU WALK AROUND THE NEIGHBORHOOD AND PET EVERY DOG THAT PASSES

before the song continues, yet words stay around you. Poison keeps words away from you. Summers of this shit too. You record. Digital you and digital summer.

You master what little you remember how you were like. You get seven flavors of you. These seven are the closest you've gotten to you. Pills cough out exhaust.

Your hand against the screen. You unplug you and unplug the recording set up because you feel you should know you're illegal.

Cherry bones. You crack a house over your head. You crown from the combs inside. You cling to you and excavate the wound. Ideas splinter

YOU TRY TO FEEL LIKE YOURSELF
38

YOU ASK FOR HELP
80

YOU FUMBLE AN OMELETTE OVER AND END UP MAKING SCRAMBLED EGGS AND IT STILL TASTES FINE BUT IT JUST TASTES FINE

racists and insects and file
systems and percentages off
and luggage and staircases
and sundown and cigarette
butts and [change agent] and

the middle and just past the
middle and still ways to go
and turtles and frozen corn
and empty chairs and mind
blown and well tomorrow
you guess and you pull at
your outline and you feel
surprised what's happening
is really actually happening
and melted wool
and magic tricks
and laundry carts, wet
garage sales, songs sung by birds,
fuck, today, a kiss on your cheek,
summers of summers of summers

YOU BUDGET ENERGY FOR DIFFERENCES YOU WANT TO SEE
18

YOU TAP INTO MEMORIES AND BREAK A VALVE
27

YOU HELP A NEIGHBOR MOVE A LARGE DRESSER AND YOU NOD A LOT BECAUSE OF THE LANGUAGE BARRIER

closet of hands. You binge high fives. You find a note that reads how you are the cause of all of this. You're hungry. You wait in line to make a sandwich. You notice a leak.

It widens. You deflate, patching what you can with conversations. You know this about you.

You wonder what makes you stay.

Summers pass, and every day makes you forget this about you. You're your best friend. You rent video tapes weekly. These stories slip into your mouth. You strive for static eyes. You help you get there. Alarms trip over themselves.

Houses blemish your forehead. Shit glitters. You lace your future with double knots. You join a company meant to help you. It disbands by mid-morning. The day wears itself in the mirror.

You blush through years. You knock you out of the park. You look down with a thumbs up. Your stomach drops as you leave. More alarms. The house announces the time. Everyone is done. You help each other up. You shake hands and just go home and get through the god damned night. Tomorrow is motherly. You start from a good place to confront yourself. Lily milkshakes. Moss. Hound.

Maple.

You learn useful things about yourself. You adapt. Bedrooms seem to sing without you. You find purpose as treasurer of a group dedicated to hating yourself. Barbecue. Next summer cools this summer with last summer.

You're the new

YOU SPILL SECRETS INTO A FAN IN A ROBOT VOICE
23

YOU TRY TO FEEL LIKE YOURSELF
38

YOU BAKE EXCUSES FOR YOUR AVOIDANCE

the house in bloom, grazing, hours, throughout. The world calls out to you, and you listen attentively. You feel it's like home with an extra step to it all. The day jerks you back, and you seek to make today then with what's around you. You dig through outlets and wires, wires, seeds. These piles fill the home. Monstrous. You come across this. You distribute wires and seeds to help you. You pull to be beyond you. Stunt, willow, late bills, good nights - replaced with today.

You spot light in summers in bottles you suck. You flicker.

Boredom. Intense fear.

Mist.

You share with you the window where light spatters with color. You fold this moment into your pocket. You wash it on accident that weekend. It sheds and sticks to you. The moment becomes a nuisance, and you feel relief in cleaning the whole experience away. You take you away. You hold you accountable for whatever happened to you.

You wrap the house in a trash bag and throw it away. You told yourself you'd do more today, and today makes this exciting. The morning waits in bed to nuzzle longer.

You rush. Hundreds complain and block your way back. You overwhelm you. Trumpets announce you, freezing the crowd. You pass. You forget the whole thing. Oat, cigarettes, you only leave now to come back. Smoothies, chalk, prison. Shades spread buttered across the floor, over rooms.

Lines skid, worn with ware.

Layers concentrate. Hours grate

YOU FUMBLE AN EMELETTE OVER AND END UP MAKING SCRAMBLED EGGS AND IT STILL TASTES FINE BUT IT JUST TASTES FINE
73

YOU SPEND A NIGHT THINKING ABOUT THE DAY AFTER WITHOUT PANIC AND WITHOUT FEAR AND WITHOUT CONCERN AND WITHOUT JUDGEMENT AND WITHOUT DOUBT
28

YOU LEAVE CHANCES TO DRY

conversations that simmer. You stand next to you and mock you with your hand clasped. You unplug you before a fight breaks out. You take you and make each other embrace the other. You find it impossible to change the expressions.

You feel you can look otherwise.

You spend summers learning how to make masks out of objects in the house, what you leave around the house.

You wrap these and unwrap them as gifts for yourself.

You hand these out to you, and you mock them. You break out into a fight. You push you to the ground, and you lay there, in the middle, for summers, counting dots in the ceiling, losing count, and starting again.

Summers of restarts.

You take the mask, and, even though you mocked them, you wear it at night when you feel no one is looking. At night, you don't know and try not to care. Basketball and bus routes, hip hop and cum, you're the neighbor

YOU TAKE A SUMMER
5

YOU WAKE UP TOMORROW
24

YOU MUNCH TELEVISION SHOWS

babies, almond, you feel mildly haunted. You hear the house whisper. You feel jealous when the house whispers to you. You remember remembering how these words felt. You pick up your agenda for the day. You route the day based on what you know of the house.

You unplug you. You make a routine of finding the sockets. It's easier to just pull from the source, yet you take pride in seeing who you are before you unplug you. This means summers of following, summers of seeing. You see and follow summers of wires, extension cords, and power strips to you. You do this all for you. You tell yourself this for summers.

You creek much more this summer,

**YOU BAKE EXCUSES FOR
YOUR AVOIDANCE
76**

**YOU WAKE UP
TOMORROW
24**

YOU ASK FOR HELP

you find yourself only here when shit gets louder.

Fat petals. Gloss brow. A butcher knife with butterfly wings. You find comfort against you. Then you ask fit your signature. You were afraid all these summers were for this moment. In your head, you always knew. It had just been so much more before the original intention returned and finished as coldly as it has started. You sign your signature. This shell for summers.

Goddammit. You drank a fridge full of summers in minutes. The house shutters. You all understand.

You all tear you apart. Moments as shapes that work together. This new place is everything in the light. You don't know how to live here though. You suffer.

Tamale, last summer, soda, calendars. Raspberry ice cream. Tenderloin.

You run away.

You dash up a hill of you applauding and jump at the floating ladder. You feel you ruined your only chance to change. You see it all, look around you, how you've come apart, and get to work. Training wheels. Loud potatoes.

Microscopes studying all your mistakes. The house simmers for summers. You recycle and throw the excess to every television show you can think of. You build weeks around watching these. You ask if you can do more for yourself. You haven't spoken for summers. You unplug yourself.

Roulette, underwear, your attention rusts. The mechanic in your head asks for help. You wait for deliveries for summers. You find yourself in waiting. You see you and grab your attention. You gather a small crowd. You peel at your husk. You follow shortly. You look with disgust.

You know what looks like not needing needs the most.

And you better not get in your way because you'll kick the fucking shit out of you for slowing you down.

Because fuck you.

You find hope in being with you. In your head, that summer pauses for summers. Because you're important to you. Ever since

YOU TAKE A SUMMER
5

YOU WAKE UP TOMORROW
24

YOU NOTHING AND NOTHING ELSE

coaches, flour, gasoline, sneezes. You find minutes in the grass. You store these in sandwich bags. The fridge is full of minutes and summers.

This summer tells you you're your own fault.

You follow a wire along the side of the house.

It's bright and misty out.

You pull yourself onto the roof. Puddles tower.

You feel the house alive beneath you. The wire stretches into the sky. You hold onto it with one hand and dunk your other into the water. Houses scatter houses across lawns across the neighborhood. Handfuls into wicker baskets. An extra thing in your head.

You wet your face. Colors chase each other. You document these with photos. You know, if colors exist, you do too.

Water lurches. You rip the wire with you, into, through depths, rushing, towing the day, halted, seconds, minutes restless in the fridge, shoving, shattering summers. These bags migrate. Lights die. Plugs faint over rooftops.

Hands spiral from soot. Fingers wire

YOU THANK THE DAY
30

YOU MOVE FURNITURE
BECAUSE THESE ARE THE
CHANGES YOU FEEL YOU
NEED TO FEEL NEW
12

YOU FORGE A NEW PERSONALITY

while each day lays on the carpet. The summer in days, these days in years. You leave the house and stay behind while you walk away. You mostly just wish you'd stay forever. You say you're just different.

Your tongue whines for leather. You always get you in the mail.

Water towers over houses around the house. You wonder how far you'll go.

Razzle dazzle. You reunion. You form a committee.

You take inventory of each summer in bottles in the fridge. You organize these by date by preference by value by geography in rations. You concoct a sign-in sheet.

Sometimes you escape you. When you're close to you, you let you grab you a summer, and you take this opportunity to take a summer for yourself. You spent an afternoon sharing the next few weeks with you.

Tomorrow to get by. You were told that blossoms were in season. Hoots and hollers scatter across the dining room table, and you're over these sounds in thr house. You're mad at yourself making these sounds in this house while you sit on the floor, just out of reach of the sun through the window.

These refractions on the floor name themselves by begging.

Cocaine.

You lead you away for this. You share what you can. There's pressure pulsing in your head. You feel you're on the verge of giving. Knock-knock jokes, belt.

You learn you can give yourself to a tiny house. You follow a list of needs and try to provide them. There's you who develops techniques and data, then there's you in it and adapting and grinding down. You find stability seesawing between the two in the middle of flux of change.

Rosemary, drains. Your lungs fill with balloons. The house points. You sleep against the ceiling, dreaming about being away from the house; ignorant, anti-what-you-have-known. Foliage dioramas, grinning,

YOU DON'T FEEL LIKE YOU AND YOU CAN'T MAKE YOU HAPPEN
53

YOU TAKE A SUMMER
5